The flying of model aircraft is recognised as a sport by the Sports Council, and the governing body of the sport is The Society of Model Aeronautical Engineers Limited. There are Model Flying Clubs in most cities and large towns. If you are interested in joining such a club, write to the following address for details of clubs in your area:

The Society of Model Aeronautical Engineers Ltd, Kimberley House, Vaughan Way, Leicester.

Contents

The publishers and author wish to acknowledge the help given by The Model Shop, Loughborough.

how to make Flying Models

written by
JULIAN COOPER

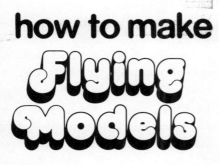

illustrated by
JULIAN COOPER

with photographs by
TIM CLARK and JOHN MOYES

Ladybird Books Loughborough

INTRODUCTION

Flying models do not always resemble full-size aircraft. They do, however, usually conform to the same basic design. Fig 1 opposite shows a small light aircraft. Marked on the photograph are the wing, tail, fuselage and fin.

The wing provides lift to enable the aircraft to fly. The tail and fin, as well as carrying control surfaces, give the aircraft stability. The fuselage carries the power unit (engine), passengers and also the wing tail and fin. The location of the wing may vary, as may the shape. To increase stability most aircraft have their wings angled upwards (*dihedral*). Most aircraft have a tail unit, although some delta-winged fighter aircraft do not need one because of the shape and section of their wings.

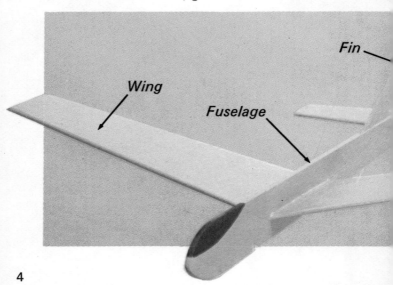

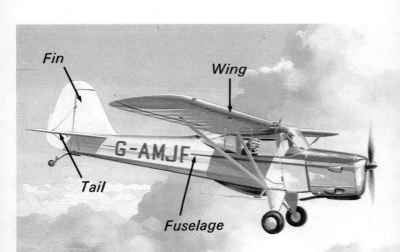

FIG. 1

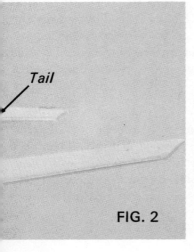

FIG. 2

Fig 2 opposite shows a model *catapult glider*, with wing, tail, fin and fuselage marked. The model does not resemble the full-size aircraft, although it still retains the same basic design.

How an aeroplane flies

Before we begin to make the model we must first understand how and why an aeroplane flies.

We know that all aircraft, whether models or full size, are heavier than air, so that to stay in the air (to *sustain flight*) they must always be moving forward. The wing of an aircraft must create *lift* to stop the aircraft diving into the ground.

In **Fig 1,** a flat board is being pushed forward through the air. The lines show the airflow along the upper and lower surfaces. The only effect is a small amount of resistance caused by the frontal area of the board parting the airflow.

In **Fig 2,** a flat board with the front edge raised is being pushed forward through the air. The under-surface of the board now presents a greater frontal area, and more resistance is caused. This makes the airflow push against the under-surface of the board. The airflow over the upper surface of the board breaks away from the surface (as shown by the lines) and a decrease in air pressure occurs. This has the effect of sucking the wing upwards.

In **Fig 3,** the upper surface has been curved (*cambered*) to increase the effect shown in Fig 2. The effect of the decreased pressure 'sucking' on the upper surface, and the increased pressure on the lower surface, caused the wing to rise when moving forward.

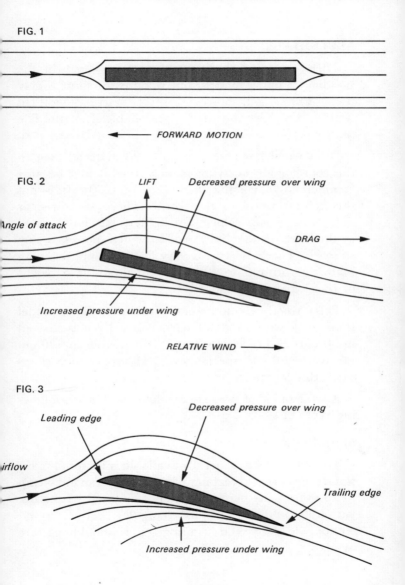

FIG. 1

FORWARD MOTION

FIG. 2

Angle of attack

LIFT

Decreased pressure over wing

DRAG

Increased pressure under wing

RELATIVE WIND

FIG. 3

Leading edge

Decreased pressure over wing

Airflow

Trailing edge

Increased pressure under wing

MATERIALS

There are several different materials used in the building of flying models, but wood is the most widely used. The wood, however, must be very light in weight, but must also have a reasonable strength. The most suitable wood with these qualities is balsa wood.

Balsa wood has been the standard material used in the construction of flying models since it first became commercially available in the early 1930s. It is not the lightest wood in the world. There are three or four other woods which are lighter, but balsa wood is the first of the light woods which possesses any strength. The balsa tree is very fast growing, reaching maturity within 7 to 10 years and attaining a height of 18–27 metres (60–90 ft).

Balsa wood is commercially available from model shops in a wide range of sizes. Normally it is stocked in 90 cm (36 in) lengths but it is available in 120 cm (48 in) lengths to special order, although some shops stock this length.

A wide range of sizes are available within the following types of stock.

Strip Sizes

The smallest size generally available is 1.5 mm ($\frac{1}{16}$ in) square. Square and rectangular sections are available up to 25 mm (1 in) across. As well as normal strip sizes, various mouldings such as triangular section, round section, leading and trailing edge mouldings are available.

BALSA STRIP SIZE CHART

	1.5 mm ($\frac{1}{16}$ in)	2 mm ($\frac{3}{32}$ in)	3 mm ($\frac{1}{8}$ in)	4 mm ($\frac{3}{16}$ in)	6 mm ($\frac{1}{4}$ in)	8 mm ($\frac{3}{8}$ in)	12 mm ($\frac{1}{2}$ in)	18 mm ($\frac{3}{4}$ in)	25 mm (1 in)
1.5 mm ($\frac{1}{16}$ in)	■		■	■	■				
2 mm ($\frac{3}{32}$ in)		■							
3 mm ($\frac{1}{8}$ in)	■		■	■	■	■	■		
4 mm ($\frac{3}{16}$ in)	■		■	■	■	■			
6 mm ($\frac{1}{4}$ in)	■				■	■			■
8 mm ($\frac{3}{8}$ in)			■		■	■	■		
12 mm ($\frac{1}{2}$ in)				■		■	■		
18 mm ($\frac{3}{4}$ in)								■	
25 mm (1 in)					■		■		■

Size available ■   Size not available ☐

BALSA STRIP MOULDINGS

TRAILING EDGES

LEADING EDGES

   TRIANGULAR

   CIRCULAR

Sheet Sizes

Sheet stock is usually sold in various thicknesses 75 mm (3 in) wide, although it is available 100 mm (4 in) and 50 mm (2 in) wide in some shops. Stock sizes vary in thickness from 0.75 mm ($\frac{1}{32}$ in) up to 12 mm ($\frac{1}{2}$ in).

Block Sizes

Block sizes are those sizes stocked above 25 mm square. Most shops are prepared to cut block sizes to the length required by the model builder, because of the high cost of a 90 cm (36 in) length of these sizes.

Balsa wood, although very light in weight, may vary greatly. Soft pithy balsa wood is very light but is also weak. Hard balsa wood is comparatively heavy, but is also very strong. Model builders usually choose the grade of wood most suited to their purpose.

In certain high stress areas, harder woods may be used, or used to supplement balsa wood. Spruce and obeche are both widely available in strip and sheet sizes. Since they are about four times as heavy as medium grade balsa wood, they are used only where balsa wood is too weak.

In areas where very high strength is required, harder woods may have to be used. Ramin and beech are available in strip sizes. Where a harder sheet wood is required, plywood is the material most widely used. It is available in thicknesses from 0·75 mm ($\frac{1}{32}$ in) to 12 mm ($\frac{1}{2}$ in). Ramin and plywood are sold at most Do-It-Yourself shops.

ADHESIVES

There are many different types of adhesives available to the model maker. Some adhesives are only suitable for gluing one type of material whilst others will stick almost anything. Balsa wood is readily glued by a wide variety of adhesives.

1 Balsa cement

This is a cellulose-based adhesive which, as its name implies, is specifically made for gluing balsa wood. Balsa cement is very fast drying and as such enables models to be built very quickly. However, there are several disadvantages to using balsa cement. Because of its fast drying qualities, it is not suitable for laminating or assembling large pieces, as the cement invariably dries before the whole joint is coated. When gluing end grains of balsa wood, it is necessary to pre-cement the joint, as the cement penetrates deeply into the wood. Balsa cement shrinks on drying and as a result may warp delicate model structures.

2 PVA (Poly-vinyl-acetate) glues

This range of adhesives is the main rival to balsa cement. The glues are almost invariably a white thick liquid, which dries by the evaporation of the water base. As they are water-based, PVA glues are not waterproof. They are slower drying than balsa cements, and are very suitable for laminating or assembling large pieces. There is no shrinkage on drying and this makes them useful for light, delicate model structures. Pre-cementing joints is not necessary.

	BALSA CEMENT	PVA GLUES	IMPACT-ADHESIVES	EPOXY RESINS	CYANO-ACRYLICS
STRIP BALSA TO STRIP BALSA	Suitable	Most suitable	May be used	Not suitable	Not suitable
LAMINATING STRIP AND SHEET BALSA	May be used	Most suitable	Suitable	Not suitable	Not suitable
STRIP AND SHEET BALSA TO HARDWOOD OR PLYWOOD	Suitable	Most suitable	Suitable	May be used	Not suitable
HARDWOOD OR PLYWOOD TO HARDWOOD OR PLYWOOD	Suitable	Most suitable	Not suitable	May be used	May be used
BALSA, PLYWOOD OR HARDWOOD TO METAL	Not suitable	Not suitable	Not suitable	Most suitable	Suitable
METAL TO METAL	Not suitable	Not suitable	Not suitable	Most suitable	Suitable
JOINT REINFORCING	Suitable	Not suitable	Not suitable	Most suitable	May be used
FIELD REPAIRS	Suitable	Not suitable	Not suitable	Most suitable	Suitable

MOST SUITABLE

SUITABLE

MAY BE USED

NOT SUITABLE

3 Impact adhesives

This group of adhesives has a very limited use in the building of flying models. They may be used for sheet and strip lamination, and are more suitable if they are thinned with cellulose thinners so that they can be brushed on to the joints.

4 Epoxy resins

These adhesives áre two-part adhesives, and are usually sold in packs of two tubes. One tube contains the resin adhesive and the other tube contains a chemical hardener. Usually equal amounts are squeezed out of the two tubes and mixed together. The glue sets as a result of the chemical reaction which starts when the two parts are mixed together. This range of adhesives can be split into two distinct types: (a) fast drying – these are dry in times varying from four minutes to thirty minutes; and (b) slow drying – these are dry in times varying from six to twenty-four hours.

The slow-drying varieties give the strongest joint but the time factor may be too great if the joint is required quickly. The slow-drying varieties may be speeded up by applying heat.

5 Cyano-acrylic adhesives

This range of adhesives is the most recent addition to the types of adhesives available to the model builder. There are various types available, some being two-part. Cyano-acrylics set in the absence of oxygen.

They set instantly in most cases, and will stick almost anything together permanently. Because of this, they can be *very dangerous* and must be handled with great care. Gluey fingers will stick together instantly and will need to be separated with a scalpel – by a doctor! The glue will also join any other two objects if drips occur. Minimum quantities should be used and absolutely clean working at all times is essential. In spite of these dangers, cyano-acrylics are a very useful addition to a modeller's equipment, if treated with respect.

TOOLS

Modelling knife

Modelling knives are sold in a wide range of shapes and sizes, and choice is very much a matter of personal preference. Light slim-handled knives are best for cutting small wood sizes, whilst a knife with a heavier and stouter blade is suited to heavier work.

Most modelling knives are usually sold with a straight, tapered, pointed end single-edged blade. This is ideal for general work but for special jobs, different blade shapes are available. Gouges, punches and special carving blades are all obtainable and are invaluable for their special shapes. For cutting large sheet and block sizes, some knives can be fitted with a razor saw blade.

Razor blades

Razor blades are generally thinner and sharper than most modelling knives, and many modellers use them.

They are however very brittle and it is very easy to cut yourself with the double-edged kind, so we do not recommend them. The stiff-backed razor blades are safer but we do not recommend their use either.

Ruler and straight edge

Metal rulers, although expensive, are the most suitable rulers for use in model building. Being metal, they may also be used as a straight edge for cutting purposes. Plastic or wooden rulers may be used for ruling and drawing, but must not be used for cutting as they quickly become damaged by the blade.

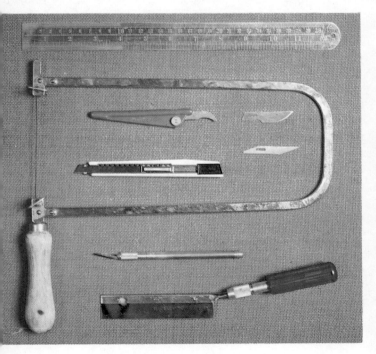

Modelling pins

Special modelling pins are sold by model shops. The pins have round glass heads which are easily gripped to push the pins into the building board. Dressmaker's pins may be used. They are sold in boxes or on cards and are less expensive than the glass-headed modelling pins.

Sanding block

Inexpensive sanding blocks made of cork are available from most Do-It-Yourself shops.

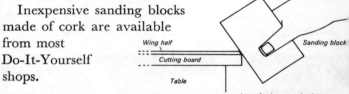

chamfering technique

Sandpaper

Sandpaper or glasspaper is sold in a wide variety of grades at most hardware stores and model shops. The slightly more expensive garnet paper lasts longer, as the wood dust does not clog the abrasive surface.

BUILDING BOARD

Flying models, whether built from plans or kits, are usually built on a building board. This must be flat and rigid, without any tendency to bend. Sizes of building boards vary, but an ideal size is 90 cm (36 in) long and 50 cm (20 in) wide cut from 12 mm ($\frac{1}{2}$ in) plywood. The thick plywood makes a good rigid base, but to be used as a building board it must be possible to push pins into the surface, without having to resort to using a hammer. One way to do this is to cut a piece of builders' insulation board to the same size as the base board, and glue it to the top surface using contact adhesive. Builders' insulation board is a soft compressed board about 12 mm ($\frac{1}{2}$ in) thick, and is sold quite cheaply at most wood merchants.

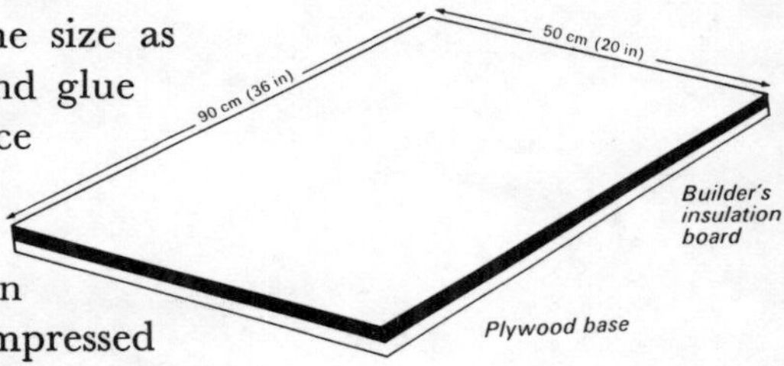

90 cm (36 in)

50 cm (20 in)

Builder's insulation board

Plywood base

CUTTING BOARD

The soft surface of the building board would soon become damaged if it was used for cutting out model aircraft parts. It is necessary to make a separate board for this purpose. Hard woods such as plywood and hardboard around 3 mm ($\frac{1}{8}$ in) thick are ideally suited to this purpose. The cutting board should not be too large and a reasonable size would be 45 cm (18 in) by 25 cm (10 in).

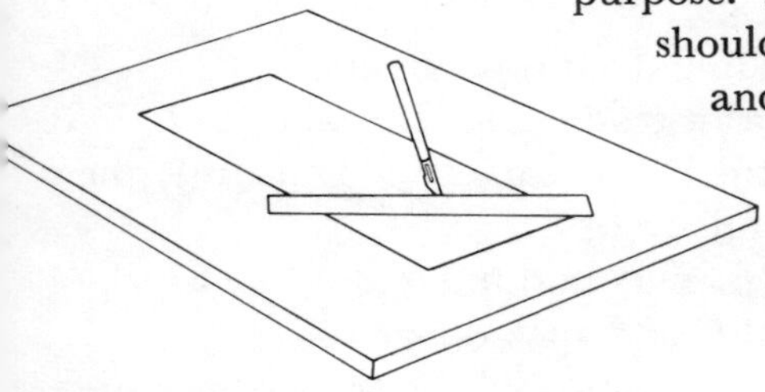

Fretsaw

A fretsaw is required when cutting complicated shapes out of larger sheet sizes and hard woods such as plywood.

PAPER PLANE

You will need:

> *one piece of writing (type) paper 28 cm by 20 cm*
> *(11 in by 8 in)*
> *scissors*
> *PVA glue*

The design may be flown outdoors on a calm day.

1 Study the folding diagrams carefully.

2 Using Fig 1 as a guide, fold the paper in half to give a size of 10 cm by 28 cm (4 in by 11 in), then open out again to full size.

3 Fold the top corners into the middle. Coat edges shown with PVA glue and stick down.

4 Using Fig 2 as a guide, fold the corners indicated on the diagram into the centre. Coat the edges shown with PVA glue and stick down as in Fig 3.

5 Using Fig 3 as a guide, fold the model along the centre line with all the folds on the inside.

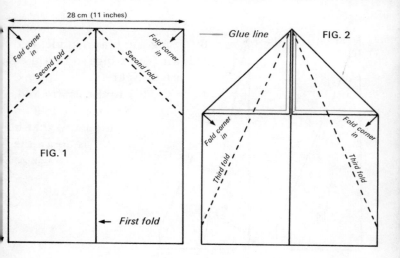

28 cm (11 inches)

Fold corner in

Second fold

FIG. 1

First fold →

Glue line — FIG. 2

Fold corner in

Second fold

Fold corner in

Third fold

Fold corner in

Third fold

6   Using Fig 4 as a guide, fold both wings in half down the fold line as shown in the diagram. Allow the wings to return to the position shown in Fig 4.

7   Using Fig 5 as a guide, mark out the line to cut along. The line should be 2 cm ($\frac{3}{4}$ in) in from the back edge of the bottom fold and 5 cm (2 in) in from the back on the centre fold. Cut along the line formed by these points.

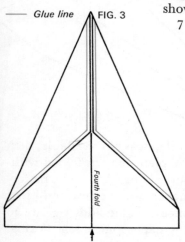

Glue line — FIG. 3

Fourth fold

Fold in half along this line

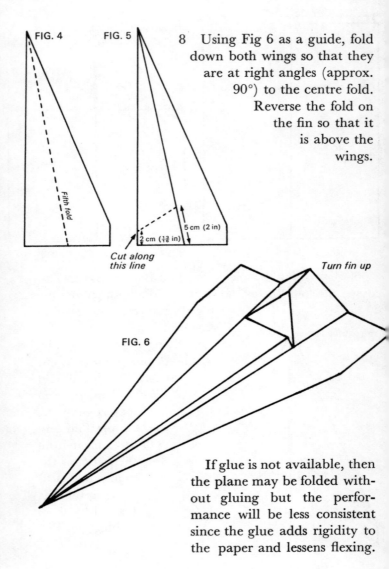

FIG. 4

FIG. 5

Fifth fold

5 cm (2 in)

2 cm (1¾ in)

Cut along this line

FIG. 6

Turn fin up

8 Using Fig 6 as a guide, fold down both wings so that they are at right angles (approx. 90°) to the centre fold. Reverse the fold on the fin so that it is above the wings.

If glue is not available, then the plane may be folded without gluing but the performance will be less consistent since the glue adds rigidity to the paper and lessens flexing.

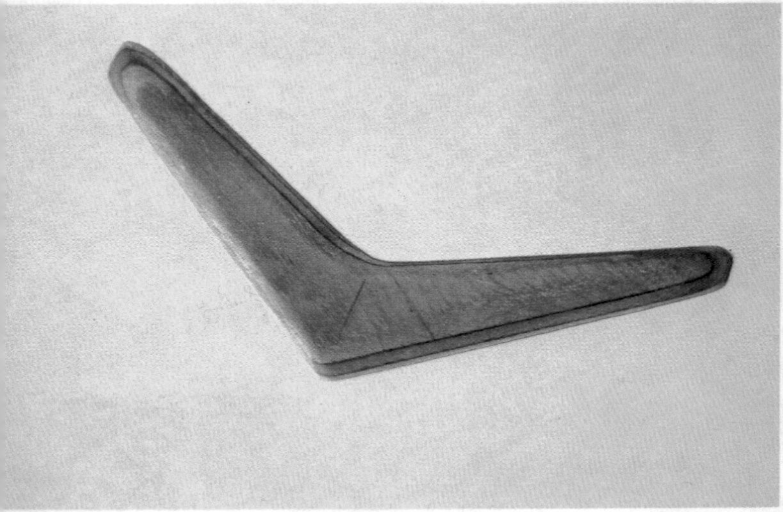

BOOMERANG

How to make

1 Study the drawing carefully and enlarge the plan to full size, using the dimensions shown.

2 Trace or draw the shape of the boomerang onto 3 mm ($\frac{1}{8}$ in) plywood.

3 Cut out the boomerang using a fretsaw, and sandpaper the edges to shape.

4 The upper surface of the blades must be shaped to the section shown in the diagram. Be sure to shape the leading and trailing edges on each blade correctly as any mistake will prevent the boomerang from working correctly. The shaping is easily done using a

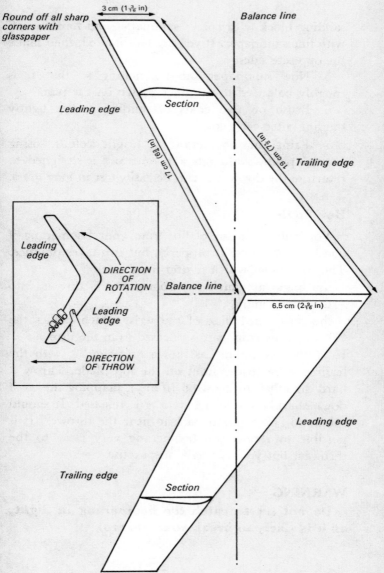

Round off all sharp corners with glasspaper

3 cm (1 3/16 in)

Balance line

Leading edge

Section

17 cm (6 3/4 in)

19 cm (7 1/2 in)

Trailing edge

Leading edge

DIRECTION OF ROTATION

Leading edge

Balance line

6.5 cm (2 9/16 in)

DIRECTION OF THROW

Leading edge

Trailing edge

Section

sanding block with coarse sandpaper and finishing off with fine sandpaper. If you are left-handed, then shape the opposite sides.

5 Now sandpaper the boomerang so that it is roughly balanced to the lines shown on the plan.

6 Brush on two coats of sanding sealer, lightly sanding after each coat.

7 Paint the boomerang a bright colour, using enamel paint. Although a boomerang is designed to return to the thrower it can be easily lost in long grass.

How to fly

You will get a lot of fun from your boomerang if you learn to throw it properly, but this takes practice. The two things which matter most are:

the angle at which the boomerang is thrown into the wind; and

the downward flick of the wrist which makes the boomerang spin as it is released from the throw.

Hold the boomerang as shown on page 23, with the leading edge to the front on the top blade. Throw it hard directly into the wind (if any), snapping the wrist down sharply as the boomerang is released. It should spin, and curve round back to near the thrower. It is possible to return the boomerang very close to the thrower: but you *will* have to practise.

WARNING

Do not try to catch the boomerang in flight, as it is likely to break your fingers.

CATAPULT GLIDER

This design is a very simple catapult glider which is launched using a length of rubber (elastic band). The design may be used as a chuck glider if you wish.

How to make

1 Study the drawing carefully and enlarge the plan to full size, using the dimensions shown. Read through the building instructions carefully.

2 Trace or draw the shape of the wing onto a sheet of medium grade 1.5 mm ($\frac{1}{16}$ in) balsa wood and cut round the outline using a straight edge and a modelling knife. Do not cut the wing in half.

3 Round off the leading and trailing edges of the wing, using fine grade sandpaper. Cut the wing in

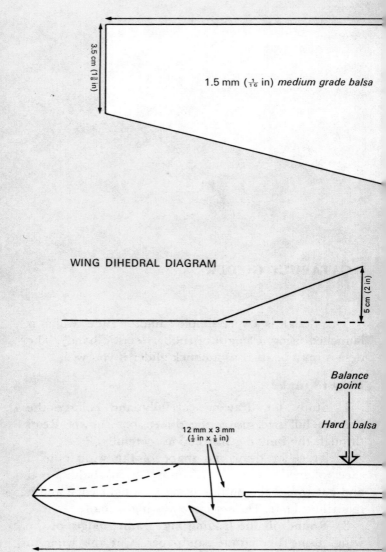

3.5 cm (1⅜ in)

1.5 mm (1/16 in) *medium grade balsa*

WING DIHEDRAL DIAGRAM

5 cm (2 in)

Balance point

Hard balsa

12 mm x 3 mm (½ in x ⅛ in)

28 cm (11 in)

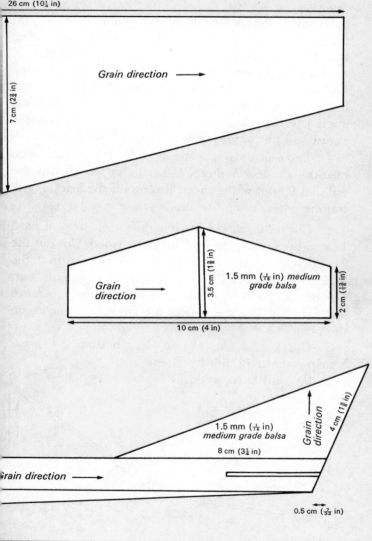

26 cm (10¼ in)

7 cm (2¾ in)

Grain direction →

Grain direction →

3.5 cm (1⅜ in)

1.5 mm (1/16 in) *medium grade balsa*

2 cm (¾ in)

10 cm (4 in)

1.5 mm (1/16 in) *medium grade balsa*

4 cm (1⅝ in)

Grain direction ↑

8 cm (3¼ in)

Grain direction →

0.5 cm (3/32 in)

half down the centre line, and chamfer the joint using a sanding block and the edge of the cutting board (see page 16). Pin one half of the wing flat on the building board. Coat the centre joint of each wing half with PVA glue. Pack up the tip of the other wing half by 5 cm (2 in). (This ensures the correct dihedral angle.) When the wing is dry, remove it from the board and put to one side.

4   Trace or draw the shape of the tail and fin onto medium grade 1.5 mm ($\frac{1}{16}$ in) balsa wood. Cut the tail and fin out of the sheet. Round off the leading and trailing edges, using fine grade sandpaper.

5   Cut a 28 cm (11 in) length from a strip of hard 12 mm by 3 mm ($\frac{1}{2}$ in by $\frac{1}{8}$ in) balsa wood. Cut out the 3.5 cm ($1\frac{3}{8}$ in) slot for the tail making sure that the knife is held vertically, thus ensuring a 'square' cut. Cut out the 7 cm by 1.5 mm ($2\frac{3}{4}$ in by $\frac{1}{16}$ in) clearance for the wing. Cut the rear of the fuselage as shown on the plan.

6   Cut a 27.5 cm ($10\frac{3}{4}$ in) length from a strip of hard 12 mm by 3 mm ($\frac{1}{2}$ in by $\frac{1}{8}$ in) balsa wood.

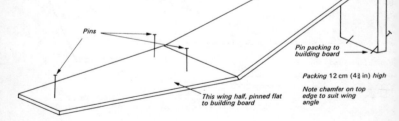

Pins

Pin packing to building board

Packing 12 cm (4$\frac{3}{4}$ in) *high*

Note chamfer on top edge to suit wing angle

This wing half, pinned flat to building board

7 Coat both fuselage halves with PVA glue along the joint edge. Pin both halves together flat on the building board.

8 When the fuselage assembly is dry, cut the fuselage bottom in half diagonally, as shown on the plan. Cut the catapult notch in the underside and round off the nose, using medium grade sandpaper.

9 Coat the tail/fuselage joint with PVA glue, and slide the tail into position. Make sure the trailing edge of the tail is at right angles (90°) to the fuselage, and that the assembly is 'square'. If necessary, pin the tail in position until the joint is dry.

10 Coat the fin/fuselage joint with PVA glue and place the fin in position, making sure that the fin is vertical and in a straight line down the middle of the fuselage. If necessary, pin the fin in position until joint is dry.

11 Coat the wing/fuselage joint with PVA glue and slide the wing through the slot into position. Run PVA glue down both sides of the joint. Ensure that the trailing edge of the wing is at right angles (90°) to the fuselage and that the wing dihedral is equal both sides of the fuselage. Use pins to ensure the correct positioning of the wing until the assembly is dry.

12 When the airframe is dry, check the alignment of the model to ensure that all the parts are fitted correctly.

13 Brush on the airframe two coats of sanding sealer, lightly sanding after each coat. Decorate the model to your own colour scheme, using enamel paint.

How to fly

1 Push a pin into the top of the fuselage at the balance point shown on the plan. Suspend the model from the pin, using sewing thread. Add 'Plasticine' to the nose of the model until the fuselage is horizontal. Remove the model from the thread and pin. The model is now ready to test.

2 Choose a calm day to test fly your model. Launch it into the wind horizontally. If the model 'dives', then remove a small amount of 'Plasticine' from the nose and try again. Repeat this until a gentle glide is achieved. If the model 'stalls', then add a small amount of 'Plasticine' to the nose, and test glide again. Repeat this until a gentle glide is achieved.

3 Lightly bend the rear of the fin to the left when holding the model with the nose forward. Be very careful not to split the wood. Test glide the model again. A slow left-hand turn on the glide should be the result.

4 To fly this model correctly, you will need at least two rubber bands 3 mm ($\frac{1}{8}$ in) wide and 7.5 cm (3 in) long. These are joined together as shown in the photo on page 40 and one end is attached to a suitable stick. (An old pencil is suitable.)

5 The model should be launched at 45° to the vertical, with the right wing banked down. The model will climb, roll out at the top of the climb, and glide in gentle left-hand turns.

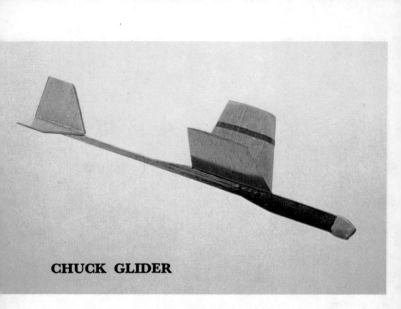

CHUCK GLIDER

This design is a simple chuck glider which is launched by hand.

How to make

1 Study the drawing carefully and enlarge the plan to full size, using the dimensions shown. Read through the building instructions carefully.

2 Trace or draw the shape of the wing onto a sheet of 3 mm ($\frac{1}{8}$ in) medium grade balsa wood. Cut round the outline of the wing using a modelling knife. Do not cut the wing in half.

3 Shape the upper surface of the wing to the section shown, using medium grade sandpaper wrapped around a sanding block. Finish off the surface of the wing using fine grade sandpaper.

4   Cut the wing in half down the centre joint line. Chamfer the centre joint to allow for the dihedral of the wings. Pin one half wing flat on the building board. Coat the centre joint of each wing half with PVA glue. Pack up the tip of the other wing by 10 cm (4 in). This ensures the correct dihedral angle. When the wing is dry remove from the board.

5   Trace or draw the shape of the tail and fin onto medium grade 1.5 mm ($\frac{1}{16}$ in) balsa wood, taking care to ensure the correct grain directions. Cut round the outline of the tail and fin. Round off the leading and trailing edges. Coat the tail/fin joint with PVA glue, and join, using pins to ensure the fin is vertical.

6   Cut a 30 cm (12 in) length of 4.5 mm ($\frac{3}{16}$ in) square spruce or ramin. Cut 20 cm (8 in) length of 4.5 mm ($\frac{3}{16}$ in) square hard balsa wood, and glue this (using PVA) to one side of the spruce (or ramin) with the ends flush. Use Sellotape to hold the two pieces together until the glue dries. Cut a 10 cm (4 in) length of 4.5 mm ($\frac{3}{16}$ in) square hard balsa wood and glue (using PVA) to the underside of the spruce, with the end flush with the other two pieces. Use Sellotape to keep the piece in position until the glue is dry.

7   Mark the position of the wing on the top of the fuselage. Chamfer the fuselage top piece down behind the wing position. Chamfer the fuselage bottom piece as shown on the drawing. Round off the nose area of the fuselage, using medium grade sandpaper.

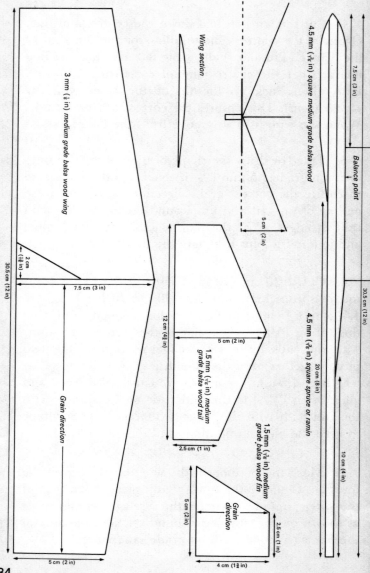

Wing section

3 mm (⅛ in) medium grade balsa wood wing

30.5 cm (12 in)

2 cm (¾ in)

7.5 cm (3 in)

Grain direction

5 cm (2 in)

4.5 mm (³⁄₁₆ in) square medium grade balsa wood

7.5 cm (3 in)

Balance point

30.5 cm (12 in)

20 cm (8 in)

5 cm (2 in)

4.5 mm (³⁄₁₆ in) square spruce or ramin

10 cm (4 in)

12 cm (4¾ in)

5 cm (2 in)

1.5 mm (¹⁄₁₆ in) medium grade balsa wood tail

2.5 cm (1 in)

1.5 mm (¹⁄₁₆ in) medium grade balsa wood fin

5 cm (2 in)

Grain direction

2.5 cm (1 in)

4 cm (1¾ in)

34

8   Coat the tail/fuselage joint with PVA glue and attach the tail/fin unit, making sure that the tail is horizontal and that the fin is central on the fuselage.

9   When the tail/fuselage joint is dry, coat the wing/fuselage joint with PVA glue. Place the wing in position – it will be necessary to pin it in position until the glue is dry. Ensure that the wing centre line is in line with the centre of the fuselage, and that the dihedral is equal on both sides.

10   When the airframe is dry, check the alignment of the model to ensure that all the parts are fitted correctly.

11   Brush on two coats of sanding sealer, lightly sanding after each coat. Decorate the model to your own colour scheme, using enamel paint.

How to fly

1   Push a pin into the top of the fuselage at the balance point shown on the plan. Suspend the model from the pin, using sewing thread. Add 'Plasticine' to the nose of the model until the fuselage is horizontal. Remove the thread and pin from the model. The model is now ready to test.

2   Choose a calm day to test fly your model, and launch it into the wind horizontally. If it 'dives', then remove a small amount of 'Plasticine' from the nose and try again. Repeat this until a gentle glide is achieved. If the model 'stalls', then add a small amount of 'Plasticine' to the nose and test glide again. Repeat this until a gentle glide is achieved.

3   Lightly bend the rear of the fin to the left when holding the model with the nose forward, being careful not to split the wood. Test glide the model again. A slow left-hand turn on the glide should result.

4   The model should be launched at 45° to the vertical, with the right-hand wing banked down. The model, when thrown, will climb, roll out at the top of the climb, and glide down in gentle left-hand turns.

FLYING FISH

This model is designed as a 'fun' model rather than a model that is meant to fly any great distance.

How to make

1 Study the drawing carefully and enlarge the drawing to full size, using the grid method of enlargement. Read through the building instructions carefully.

2 Trace or draw the shape of the wing onto a sheet of 2 mm ($\frac{3}{32}$ in) medium grade balsa wood, taking care to ensure the correct grain direction. Cut round the outline of the wing using a modelling knife. Do not cut the wing in half.

3 Round off the leading and trailing edges of the wing, using medium grade sandpaper.

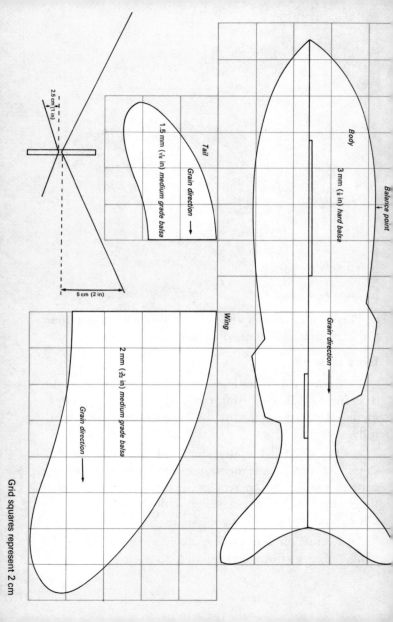

Grid squares represent 2 cm

Body

3 mm (⅛ in) hard balsa

Balance point

Grain direction

Tail

1.5 mm (1/16 in) medium grade balsa

Grain direction

Wing

2 mm (3/32 in) medium grade balsa

Grain direction

2.5 cm (1 in)

5 cm (2 in)

4   Cut the wing in half down the centre joint line. Chamfer the centre joint as shown on page 16 to allow for the dihedral of the wings. Pin one half of the wing flat to the building board. Coat the centre joint with PVA glue. Pack up the other wing by 10 cm (4 in), to ensure the correct dihedral angle. When the wing is dry, remove from the board.

5   Trace or draw the outline of the tail onto medium grade 1.5 mm ($\frac{1}{16}$ in) balsa wood, taking care to ensure correct grain direction. Cut round the outline and round off the upper surface leading and trailing edges, using fine grade sandpaper. Cut the tail in half down the centre joint line. Chamfer the centre joint slightly to allow for the anhedral (downwards dihedral). To allow for this, ensure that the upper surfaces of the tail halves are face-down on the board when chamfering. Pin one tail half to the board with the underside showing. Coat the centre joint with PVA glue and pack up the other tip by 5 cm (2 in). When dry, remove the tail from the building board.

6   Trace or draw the outline of the fuselage onto 3 mm ($\frac{1}{8}$ in) hard balsa wood. Mark the centre line and position of the wing and tail. Cut round the outline of the fuselage. Cut down the centre line. Cut out the slots for the wing and tail. Coat the fuselage centre joint with PVA glue. Pin the two halves together flat on the building board until dry. Before gluing the wing and tail in place, it will be necessary to slightly relieve the slots to allow for the dihedral and anhedral. Coat the wing centre joint with PVA glue, and slide the wing through the fuse-

lage until the dihedral is the same on both sides of the fuselage. Coat the tail centre joint with PVA glue and slide the tail through the slot until the anhedral is the same on both sides of the fuselage.

7   When the joints are dry, check the alignment of the model to ensure that all parts are fitted correctly.

8   Brush on two coats of sanding sealer, lightly sanding with fine sandpaper after each coat. Decorate the model to your own colour scheme, using enamel paint.

How to fly

The balancing and test flying instructions are as those given for the catapult glider.

ELLIPTICHUCK

This design is a more advanced chuck glider, with a superior performance to the model already described.

How to make

1 Study the drawing carefully and enlarge the plan to full size, using the grid method for enlargement. Note the thicknesses of the wood differ slightly from the previous model.

2 The construction of this model is very similar to the chuck glider, with the following exceptions:

a There are only two pieces to the fuselage, that is, there is no balsa piece under the main spruce (or ramin).

b The dihedral of the wing is different from the previous model. The wing on this model is called *polyhedral*.

Cut out the wing from the sheet, then shape it to the section shown on the plan. Cut the wing down the centre and wingtip joint lines. Chamfer all the joints

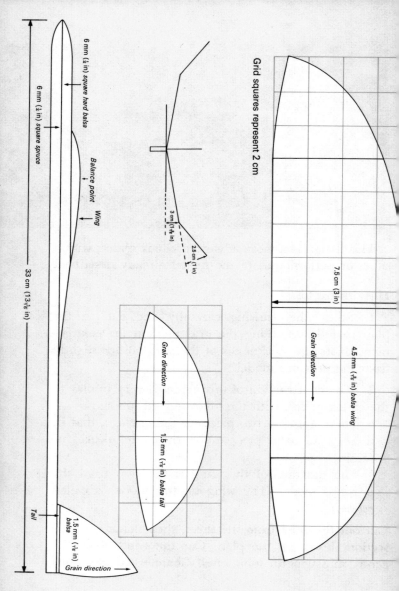

Grid squares represent 2 cm

6 mm (¼ in) square hard balsa

6 mm (¼ in) square spruce

Balance point

Wing

Tail

33 cm (13⅛ in)

3 cm (1⅛ in)

2.5 cm (1 in)

7.5 cm (3 in)

4.5 mm (³⁄₁₆ in) balsa wing

Grain direction

Grain direction

1.5 mm (¹⁄₁₆ in) balsa tail

1.5 mm (¹⁄₁₆ in) balsa

Grain direction

as shown in illustration on page 16. Pin both centre halves flat on the building board. Coat the tip joints with PVA glue and pack up the tips 2.5 cm (1 in). When the tip joints are dry, remove one wing half. Coat the centre joint with PVA glue, and join to the other wing half using 3 cm ($1\frac{3}{16}$ in) packing. When dry, remove from the board and attach to the fuselage as described for the previous model (page 35).

How to fly

The finishing, balancing and test flying of this model is also as described for the chuck glider.

BIRD MODEL

How to make

1   Study the diagrams carefully.

2   Enlarge the fuselage to full size using the dimensions shown and the grid for reference on the curved edges.

3   Draw line A from the point at the rear of the fuselage through the centre point of the circle which forms the head. Draw in line B, 1.5 cm ($\frac{5}{8}$ in) above and parallel to the centre line A. Measure in 15 cm (6 in) from the rear of the fuselage along line B. This point is the lower rear edge of the wing position. Using a protractor at this point, measure an angle of 2° as shown in the drawing, and draw in the line for the lower surface of the wing. Draw in the wing slot which is 10 cm long by 3 mm deep (4 in by $\frac{1}{8}$ in) for the basic wing shape and 9.25 cm long by 3 mm deep ($3\frac{3}{4}$ in by $\frac{1}{8}$ in) for the realistic wing shape.

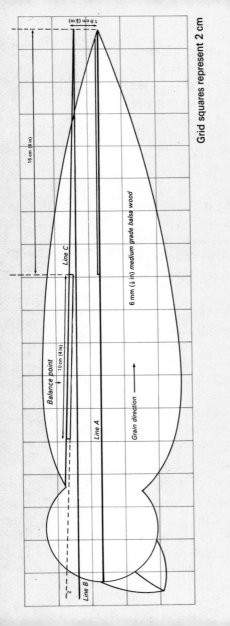

Grid squares represent 2 cm

15 cm (6 in)

1.5 cm (⅝ in)

Line C

Balance point

10 cm (4 in)

Line A

Grain direction →

6 mm (¼ in) medium grade balsa wood

Line B

2

TAIL DIHEDRAL DIAGRAM

3.5 cm (1⅜ in)

45

0.5 cm
($\frac{3}{16}$ in)

10 cm (4 in)

Grain o

4   Transfer the drawing onto a piece of 6 mm ($\frac{1}{4}$ in) medium grade balsa wood 10 cm (4 in) wide. Draw in line C as shown and cut the fuselage out of the sheet. Split the fuselage into three pieces by cutting down lines A and C.

5   Cut slots for the wing and tail positions out of the centre piece. Glue the three pieces together again using PVA adhesive, pinning the pieces flat on the building board so that when dry the joints are perfectly 'square'.

6   Enlarge the drawing of the basic wing half, to full size using the dimensions shown and the grid for reference on the tip shape. For a more realistic model, use the grid as reference to draw in the more realistic outline shown. Transfer this shape on to two pieces of 3 mm ($\frac{1}{8}$ in) medium grade balsa wood, 22 cm long by 10 cm wide ($8\frac{3}{4}$ in by 4 in).

7   Sandpaper the top surface of each wing half to the section shown. Cut the wings down the tip joint lines. Chamfer the tip joints of the centre panels as shown in the illustration on page 16, but ensure that

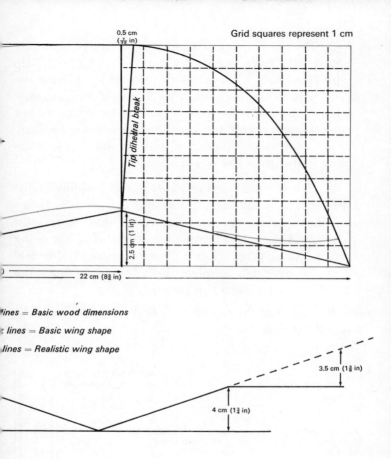

0.5 cm (3/32 in)

Grid squares represent 1 cm

Tip dihedral break

2.5 cm (1 in)

22 cm (8¾ in)

━━ lines = Basic wood dimensions

╌╌ lines = Basic wing shape

━━ lines = Realistic wing shape

3.5 cm (1¾ in)

4 cm (1¾ in)

the wing panels have their undersides facing upwards to counter the opposite effect of the tip dihedral. Turn the centre panels over so that their top surfaces are uppermost, and chamfer the centre joints.

8 Pin both wing centre panels to the building board with their undersides uppermost. Coat the tip joint lines with PVA or epoxy resin glue. Position the respective wingtips with their undersides uppermost against the joint lines. Prop up the wingtips to the correct angle using the tip dihedral props which are made from scrap 3 mm ($\frac{1}{8}$ in) balsa wood. Remove the wing halves from the board when dry.

9 Pin one wing centre panel to the building board with its top surface uppermost and the wing tip hanging downwards over the edge. Coat the centre joint with PVA or epoxy resin glue and, using the wing centre panel prop, ensure that the correct dihedral angle is achieved. Remove the whole wing from the building board when the assembly is dry.

10 Enlarge the drawing of the tail to full size using the dimensions shown.

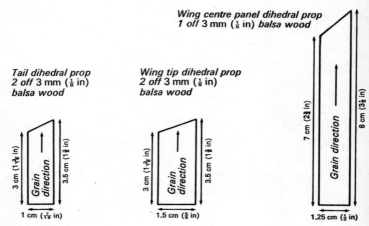

Wing centre panel dihedral prop
1 off 3 mm ($\frac{1}{8}$ in) *balsa wood*

7 cm (2$\frac{3}{4}$ in) 8 cm (3$\frac{1}{8}$ in)

Grain direction

1.25 cm ($\frac{1}{2}$ in)

Tail dihedral prop
2 off 3 mm ($\frac{1}{8}$ in) *balsa wood*

3 cm (1$\frac{3}{16}$ in) 3.5 cm (1$\frac{3}{8}$ in)

Grain direction

1 cm ($\frac{7}{16}$ in)

Wing tip dihedral prop
2 off 3 mm ($\frac{1}{8}$ in) *balsa wood*

3 cm (1$\frac{3}{16}$ in) 3.5 cm (1$\frac{3}{8}$ in)

Grain direction

1.5 cm ($\frac{5}{8}$ in)

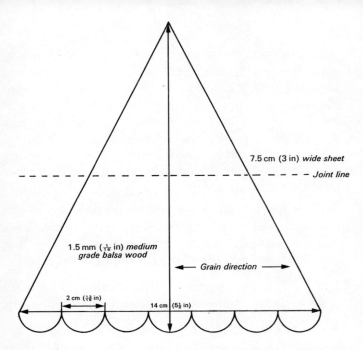

7.5 cm (3 in) *wide sheet*

– – – *Joint line*

1.5 mm ($\frac{1}{16}$ in) *medium grade balsa wood*

← *Grain direction* →

2 cm (1$\frac{3}{4}$ in)

14 cm (5$\frac{1}{2}$ in)

11   Cut two 14 cm (5$\frac{1}{2}$ in) lengths from a 7.5 cm (3 in) wide sheet of 1.5 mm ($\frac{1}{16}$ in) medium grade balsa wood. Glue the long edges of the two pieces together (use PVA adhesive), and pin on the building board until dry.

12   Transfer the outline of the tail onto the wood, and cut the tail out. Cut the tail into two pieces by cutting down the centre line. Chamfer the centre joint of each half to allow for the dihedral angle. Coat the centre joint of each half with PVA or epoxy resin adhesive, and prop up both halves with the tailplane dihedral props made from scrap 3 mm ($\frac{1}{8}$ in) balsa wood. When dry, remove from the board.

13 Smooth the fuselage outline by sandpapering with fine grade sandpaper. Coat the centre joint of the wing with PVA adhesive. Slide the wing through the wing box until the centre joint is in the centre of the fuselage. It may be necessary to slightly relieve the slot to allow for the dihedral angle of the wing. Ensure that the wing dihedral angle is equal on either side of the fuselage. If necessary, pin the wing in place until the assembly is dry.

14 Chamfer the top edges of the tail slot in the fuselage. Coat the tail/fuselage joint with PVA adhesive and slide the tail into position, ensuring that the dihedral is equal on either side of the fuselage.

15 When the assembly is dry, check the alignment of the model to ensure that all parts are fitted correctly.

16 Brush two coats of sanding sealer onto the assembly, lightly sanding after each coat. Decorate the model to your own colour scheme, using enamel paint. Bright colour schemes are best, as this model resembles a parrot in flight.

How to fly

1 Push a pin into the fuselage at the balance point shown on the drawing. Suspend the model from the pin, using sewing thread. Add 'Plasticine' to the nose of the fuselage until the fuselage is horizontal. Remove the model from the pin and thread. The model is now ready to fly.

2 Choose a calm day to test fly your model, and launch it into the wind horizontally. If the model

'dives', then remove a small amount of 'Plasticine' from the nose and try again. Repeat this until a gentle glide is achieved. If the model 'stalls', then add more 'Plasticine' to the nose and test glide again.

3   When a gentle glide has been achieved, trim the model for a gradual left turn. If the model turns too tightly in one direction, then slightly bend up the trailing edge of the opposite side of the tail, being very careful not to split the wood.

4   This model is designed as a fun flying model rather than one that will fly any great distance. Depending on the trim, the design will fly loops as well as straightforward glides. It is best to have the model turning slowly to the left on the glide.